Three Nails and a Tree

The Invisible behind the Visible in the Workplace

Roxie Hairston

iUniverse LLC
Bloomington

THREE NAILS AND A TREE
THE INVISIBLE BEHIND THE VISIBLE IN THE WORKPLACE

iUniverse books may be ordered through booksellers or by contacting:

iUniverse LLC
1663 Liberty Drive
Bloomington, IN 47403
www.iuniverse.com
1-800-Authors (1-800-288-4677)

Because of the dynamic nature of the Internet, any web addresses or links contained in this book may have changed since publication and may no longer be valid. The views expressed in this work are solely those of the author and do not necessarily reflect the views of the publisher, and the publisher hereby disclaims any responsibility for them.

Unless otherwise indicated, Scripture quotations used in this book are from the Holy Bible, King James Version.

Book Cover Designed by
Mary C. Martin, Creative Director
se7en-atl.wix.com/7

ISBN: 978-1-4917-2197-1 (sc)
ISBN: 978-1-4917-2199-5 (hc)
ISBN: 978-1-4917-2198-8 (e)

Library of Congress Control Number: 2014901644

Printed in the United States of America.

iUniverse rev. date: 02/13/2014

To Him who bore the three nails on the tree

Contents

PART FOUR
ENDING WISDOM

Introduction

Throughout the hallways every Friday, saints and sinners alike could be heard echoing, "TGIF" (Thank God it's Friday).

While conversations of weekend plans were being discussed at the water cooler, I was eagerly waiting for the short hand to land on 5 and the big hand to land on 12.

My Friday night ritual was an all—night "shut-in" with my girlfriends. It was my special time of the week to spend some "me time" with God and my girlfriends. My girlfriends and I were passionately in love with Christ, and He graciously blessed us with many of the Gifts of the Spirit that operated through each of us.

At the shut-in, we prayed, we praised, we laughed, we cried, we testified, and we shared our struggles. The Holy Spirit never disappointed; He showed up and showed out every shut-in.

In sharing our struggles, no one was ashamed or embarrassed to display her scars. Our scars were a testament that we know Christ, and the power of his resurrection, and the fellowship of his sufferings.

Before we stretched out on the floor before the Lord to begin intercessory prayer, we had the chance to ask the group to pray for a specific need in our lives. It seemed as if each week, I asked for prayer regarding the problems I was facing at work. On occasion, before I would bring up work, someone would ask how things were going on the job.

The shut-in provided a safe haven, and I took full advantage of the opportunity to "let it all hang out" when it came to disclosing the issues I was facing at work.

One Friday night when I arrived for the shut-in, the work drama had taken its toll. It was visible on my face and in my spirit. As always, my girlfriends had a listening ear. After a while, it was time to forget about work, clear our minds, and began intercessory prayer.

The night seemed to slip quickly as the burst of daylight through the windows beckoned that morning had arrived and it was time to end the shut-in. Slowly, we rose from the floor with our faces lit with a brilliance that denoted we had been in the presence of the Lord.

As we were scurrying to tidy up the place, one of my girlfriends said to me, "The Lord showed me a vision related to your struggles at work."

The vision she shared was this: "I was standing in an open field, dressed in office attire. People began to gather around me with shovels and, soon, I was standing in the middle of a large human circle. Everyone began to dig what appeared to be a ditch around me. As they scooped the earth in their shovels, they tossed the dirt on me.

When the dirt hit me, it fell from me to the ground, and I stepped on top of it and flattened it under my feet. The people digging the ditch were consumed with their task and never took the time to look at me when they threw the dirt.

At last, the people had thrown so much dirt on me, I was standing high on top of a hill looking down at them. Finally, everyone stopped digging and looked up because they heard laughter. When they looked up, I was standing high on a hill, free of dirt, laughing, and jumping for joy."

I began to sob as the Holy Spirit unveiled that the conflict at work was designed to stretch, grow, reinvent, and prune me for His use. As the Lord doesn't create overnight wonders, I knew that it was going to be a season of testing.

I began to speculate how long this process would take. Slowly, the *Rhema* word began to dissipate as I focused on me. I questioned why the Lord didn't remember how drained I was from dealing with office drama when I went to the shut-in? Why didn't He know that I was at a breaking point, and I couldn't take it anymore? As doubts swirled through my mind, I heard the Holy Spirit say, "I will be with you, and no weapons that will form against you will prevail."

That was the defining moment in which I made a decision to let God take me on this journey of spiritual transformation. During my journey, the Lord did not swoop in to rescue me at every turn. There were some dark days and lonely valleys I had to walk through.

The days of testing turned into weeks, weeks turned into months, and the months turned into years. I can recall many times asking the Lord to let me quit; telling him there is no way I will ever change into what you want me to be; or please find someone else for this experiment.

When I felt as if I was being tried in the fire for an extended period of time, I asked the Lord to take me out of the fire, but instead, He turned me over in the fire.

I kicked, I screamed, but I was also thankful for the lessons that I was learning and the changes I could see happening in me.

At times, it seemed that I was farther away than ever from the Lord and, at the same time, I sensed that there was really no distance at all separating us.

Every so often, I felt that a deep inner change had taken place, but no one seemed to have noticed any difference outwardly.

When the journey ended, I began to share with others why we face conflict in the workplace.

For believers, acquiring a job is more than a means to meet financial obligations, fulfill career aspirations, display talents, or perform workplace ministry. Most importantly, our place of employment is an avenue for the Holy Spirit to perfect the fruit of the Spirit in our lives.

Galatians 5:22-26: "But the fruit of the Spirit is love, joy, peace, longsuffering, gentleness, goodness, faith, meekness, temperance: against such there is no law. And they that are Christ's have crucified the flesh with the affections and lusts. If we live in the Spirit, let us also walk in the Spirit. Let us not be desirous of vain glory, provoking one another, envying one another."

In this book, I share biblical stories and examples that helped me as I encountered various issues in the workplace.

Using the workplace setting, the Lord changed my heart of stone into a heart of flesh. I continued to face challenges at work nevertheless; I no longer focus on what happens to me but rather what's happening within me.

None of what has been accomplished in me would be possible had it not been for the undying love and power of the One who bore the pain of three nails on a tree.

If you are in a season in which you are facing tests and trials at work, be strong in the Lord and in the power of His might. He is the invisible behind the visible in the workplace.

PART ONE

REALITY CHECK

ONE

Just a Prayer Away

Before leaving for work each day, spend time in prayer. If you take the time to put God first, nothing will suffer. Things are of less importance than you think.

Omitting prayer is the equivalent to jumping in the car with the gas hand sitting one notch from empty and believing that you don't have time to stop for gas. If you don't stop for gas, the car will stop when it has emptied its tank. Likewise, if we don't stop for prayer, our power source will empty itself.

Prayer keeps our hearts and minds throughout the day. It elevates our spiritual altitude, making our problems less magnified. Can you imagine the level of peace we would enjoy each day looking down on our problems instead of our problems bearing down upon us? We can imagine ourselves with money, the perfect mate, a good job, a nice home, but we seldom spend any time imagining spiritual success.

In an airplane thousands of feet off the ground, the cars, homes, and buildings appear small enough to hold in your hand. These objects have not shrunk; they are the same size. They appear small due to the height from which they are being viewed. This is the spiritual altitude we should walk into work with every day, ready to take on the day's challenges.

Along with your tailor-made shirts and suits, snapping gators, manicured nails as sharp as knives, and high stepping stilettos, please add prayer to your wardrobe before you show your face in the workplace.

TWO

Flow with It

I thought I had made it to the big leagues when I landed my first corporate job. I worked hard, took on new assignments, and soon others were commenting on my performance. I was focused on my job responsibilities and making sure I didn't let any balls drop; therefore, I was not aware that I had become a threat to others who had been at the company for a number of years.

In one of my weekly meetings, the manager commented that my outgoing personality, passion for excellence, and the ability to communicate effectively with others would catch the attention of key leaders who could propel me to move quickly within the organization. At the time, I didn't think anything of the comment other than it was a nice compliment.

As time passed, I noticed that the manager would abruptly change my participation in team activities and projects. I was aware of the sudden changes, but it was not a concern because I needed the extra time to focus on other areas of my work. Eventually, the changes became more frequent and obvious that my manager was trying to "stop my flow."

By the time I was in the heat of the conflict, the Holy Spirit took me to the twenty-sixth chapter of Genesis. I spent several days savoring in the wisdom of this chapter.

The spiritual insights into Isaac's conflict with the Philistines were timely. Isaac's flexibility in handling unexpected changes is a blueprint to follow when haters try to "block our flow."

When there was a famine in Canaan, the Lord spoke to Isaac and instructed him not to go into Egypt. Isaac left Canaan and went to King Abimelech in Gerar.

When he arrived in Gerar, he was afraid to disclose that his traveling companion, Rebekah, was his wife, so he introduced her as his sister.

Isaac was able to pass Rebekah off as his sister, until one day King Abimelech witnessed an interaction between

Isaac and Rebekah and realized that Isaac had lied about their relationship. Abimelech confronted Isaac about his deceit.

After he got busted, Isaac remained in Gerar and became very great. Eventually, his wealth and power alarmed the Philistines and, subsequently, King Abimelech asked Isaac to move into the valley.

Isaac left his prime piece of real estate in the city of Gerar and moved to the valley. This was a step down and a step backwards for Isaac, but with unwavering faith in God, he accepted the hand that was dealt to him.

When Isaac and his entourage arrived in the valley, they went to work. He rallied the people and gave them the confidence that everything was going to be alright even though they were starting over again.

For Isaac, finding water in the valley was his first priority. The people went to work and found a well with flowing water. Shortly after finding water, the herdsmen of Gerar and Isaac's herdsmen were in a quarrel over the water. Isaac's herdsmen felt that the water rights belonged to them because they dug the well. The herdsmen of Gerar felt that the water rights belonged to them because they were in the valley first.

The rift between the herdsmen grew so intense that Isaac made a decision to abandon the well and dig another one. Isaac walked away; he left it.

When people are adamant in standing their ground in a conflict, take the high road and let God deal with your enemies.

Isaac called the abandoned well *Esek*, which means contention. What contentions are you facing at work?

Isaac refused to engage in a fight to gain control of the well. He believed God would provide for him at his next set place; therefore, he took his faith shovel and went to dig another well.

Sometimes circumstances or people will force you to do something different than what you planned. To maintain your peace and keep focused, it is necessary, at times, to shift gears and go with the flow.

When Isaac began to dig another well, they quarreled over it, and Isaac named the well *Sitnah*, which means strife, and made the decision to abandon it.

The Philistines did not want Isaac to prosper and flourish, so they continuously caused conflict and dissention. You may be dealing right now with a co-worker or a boss who intentionally stirs up conflict and dissention with everything that you do. In the world you will have tribulation, but be of good cheer. He has overcome the world.

Isaac was then faced with moving a third time. He was willing to take more, and so can we. Once again, he trusted God to provide for him. So, without anger or hostility, he simply moved on.

When Isaac arrived at his next destination, he had no choice but to dig another well. He had to dig for water or else he would die.

Isaac set his face like a flint (i.e. made it hard, impassive, expressionless, and at the same time determined, fixed not to give way). He was unwavering that his present circumstances did not dictate his future. He saw God protect, provide, and bless him. That was good enough for him to continue trusting God even when it looked like his enemies were winning.

When it appears that your enemies are winning, God will give you peace in the midst of the chaos. God has a way of lifting the heaviness out of a burden. The problem has not gone away, but He will bring you to a place of peace and calm.

The Philistines were relishing their success in obstructing Isaac, but they didn't know that God was using them to build Isaac's character.

After Isaac and his entourage settled in Gerar for the third time, he dug another well and the Philistines left him alone. Finally, Isaac arrived in a place where there was no contention or strife. He named the well *Rehoboth*, which means "wide place."

After three attempts, Isaac found a parcel of real estate large enough for his flocks to flourish without interference from other herdsmen. God had this place prepared for Isaac before he dug his first well, but He chose to take Isaac through the conflict before he arrived at his set place of immeasurable blessings.

Sometimes God will bless you just enough to build your faith. Then it will appear as though He is silent and not doing anything. When it appears that God is not doing anything, don't faint. We walk by faith and not by our feelings or what we see.

Isaac believed that each place he tried to build a new life was the right place, even though things did not turn out as planned. We must pursue our goals and dreams even though they may not turn out the way we planned the first time, the second time, or the third.

Isaac had a winning spirit. He refused to allow what the Philistines threw at him to discourage him from digging again and again and again.

When the Philistines did not quarrel or cause trouble, Isaac said, "Now the Lord has made room for us, and we shall be fruitful."

The places in which the Philistines challenged Isaac were actually too small for him. When Isaac began to expand his territory, the Lord appeared to him and said, "I am the God of Abraham your father; fear not, for I am with you and will bless you, and multiply your seed for my servant Abraham's sake."

Notice this, God didn't speak to Isaac and give him any encouraging words while he was going through his conflict over the wells. It was not until Isaac had come through the adversity that he heard from God.

When God told Isaac to stay in Gerar, during the recession, he obeyed. When the Philistines tried to stop his flow, it did not cause his faith to waver.

There were days of little, and there were days of plenty, but when the famine ended, Isaac was a rich man. He didn't get rich because he was sitting around waiting for God to bless Him; Isaac sowed in the land.

In spite of the opposition Isaac faced, he behaved himself wisely, and, as a result, the Philistines were fearful, not of Isaac, but of Isaac's God.

In conflict, perseverance and faith in God will bring you to your Rehoboth (a wide place). When people try to block your flow, pull out your faith shovel and dig again.

THREE

Shake It Off

I worked at a mid-sized company a few years ago, and although my role was critical to the success of the company, soon I began to outgrow the job. I loved the company and did not want to leave, so I decided to look for another opportunity that matched my skills. After scanning the job board for about a month, I found a position that caught my attention.

Before applying, I reached out to an employee in the department to learn more about the position. The employee was more than generous in sharing information about the role and the team. As we were ending our conversation, the employee stated, "In addition to performing the duties of the position, one key attribute the person must possess to be successful in the role is thick skin.

As I walked away, I pondered the words "thick skin." The adage "sticks and stones may break my bones but words will never hurt me" is far from truth. The truth is—words hurt.

Without a doubt, thick skin is vital in dealing with offensive comments or criticism at work. Without thick skin, the poison in words will affect every area of our lives, adding stress during work hours and invading our spirit and thoughts outside of work. If we fail to appropriately deal with negativity, it can derail our career.

When I read the Book of Acts, I am always struck by the intensity of the harsh treatment that the Apostle Paul received from church folks.

Paul's reaction to immense opposition and conflict on the job serves as a model to follow. As we take a look at one of Paul's conflicts with the Jews, we learn countless lessons. For Paul, conflict was part of the job description, because he understood the price he had to pay for the assignment he had to execute.

Paul had a dramatic conversion experience. He was on his way to Damascus when the Lord met him and changed him. His conversion transformation was vital for his mission to carry the gospel to the Greeks and Romans.

Paul did not teach any attachments to salvation, and the Jews resented his teachings. The Jews saw him as a threat to Judaism and Christianity, because he was not teaching the Gentiles the Jewish laws and customs.

There was an incident in which the Jews became angry with Paul, so they threw him out of the church. This did not stop him; he went from house to house preaching the gospel.

One day, while at Caesarea, Agabus warned Paul that certain danger awaited him at Jerusalem. Despite the warning, Paul went to Jerusalem to report the good work of God among the Gentiles.

While at Jerusalem, certain Jews from Asia instigated a mob against Paul. The dissention flowed from inside the church to the streets. It caused an uproar and chaos. When the Roman soldiers could not ascertain the truth because of the tumult, they arrested Paul.

Paul appealed his arrest unto Caesar, using his Roman citizenship and was put on a ship to stand trial before Caesar.

While on the ship, a storm arose, causing the ship to break in pieces. The prisoners, crew, and prison guards swam safely to the island of Melita.

When they reached the island, they were cold and wet. Paul took charge and built a fire. Leaders always know what to do.

Paul had just come through a storm and needed rest and food. His strength was faint, and he wanted to light a fire and rest, but he encountered a viper in between sticks that he picked up to start a fire. He had survived the shipwreck, but the devil wasn't finished. A venomous poisonous snake fastened onto his hand and would not let it go.

The devil was not successful in drowning Paul, so he moved to Plan B; he attempted to fill Paul with poison.

Paul could not execute the will of God filled with poison. We cannot be ambassadors for Christ in the workplace loaded with jealousy, envy, bitterness, hate, anger, or resentment.

When the people on the Island of Melita saw the venomous snake attach to Paul's hand, they said among themselves, "No doubt this man is a murderer, even though he escaped death at sea, he is getting what he deserves." Take heed: someone on the job is watching how you deal with adversity.

The people on the island believed that Paul should have swollen up or fallen down dead from the snake bite, but after they observed no harm come to him, they changed their minds and said that he was a god.

On the job, we have the opportunity to change what people think of us based on how we react to adversity. We can't go through adversity and fall apart every time. The more we go through adversity, the more we should know how to handle adversity. With Christ, we should be able to come out of every storm, even if it's on broken pieces.

When the snake bit Paul, his body should have retorted with difficulty breathing, swelling, or pain. Without panicking or calling for help, he shook the snake from his hand into the fire.

We do not have to "put on blast" every attack from the enemy. Giving place to the devil opens the door for him to have a field day with us. Equally important, we should be able to go through tests and trials without having to call someone to pray for us every time we are in a storm.

The snake fastened tight onto Paul's hand and would not let go so that it could effectively release poison into him. The devil knows how to send vipers into our lives to hold us and refuse to let us go. Poison kills our attitude, our dreams, and our creativity.

As soon as someone lies about you—shake it off. As soon as they point the finger at you —shake it off. As soon as they play the game on you —shake it off. You see it—but you shake it off!

The devil wants to use the negativity from others to swell us with poison so that we will become ugly and grotesque.

If you don't shake it off, one day you will look in the mirror and wonder, who is this monster looking back at me?

FOUR

Slow Your Roll

The Word of God admonishes us not to fret ourselves because of evil doers nor be envious against the workers of iniquity. With that understanding, it can still be quite disheartening to watch individuals acquire high level positions, promotions or raises using unscrupulous tactics.

It is equally disappointing to observe Christians following the path of the ungodly to obtain success.

Those who prefer using unscrupulous tactics to climb the corporate ladder will quickly discover that it was more important to know how to stay at the top rather than how to scheme to the top.

In a work environment in which this practice is the norm, we must not allow this behavior to alter our attitude, behavior, and work ethic. We should perform our jobs as unto the Lord and not unto man. The fruit of the Spirit should be expressed through our lives even in the midst of unrighteousness.

Whether we are not chosen for a position or promotion due to favoritism or if we were intentionally overlooked, our best course of reaction should be to let it go. If we believe that our footsteps are ordered by the Lord, there is no good thing that He will withhold from us.

Letting go of offenses ensures that seeds of rejection (anger, envy, strife, jealousy, self-pity) do not fester in our spirit. Holding offenses erodes our faith and hinders God's best from flowing into our lives.

I vividly remember a teachable moment from the Holy Spirit on an occasion when I did not receive a certain promotion. My work was impeccable, I worked hard and often long hours, and made personal sacrifices, but in spite of these things, I did not get the promotion. When I found out that another employee was given the promotion, I was quite upset and elected not to release the offense right away.

I didn't say anything to the Lord but, in my heart, I wanted to know why He didn't open a door or even a window for me to acquire the promotion. I really wanted that promotion. After sulking for a day or so, I decided that my pity party had gone on long enough, and it was time to move forward.

Shortly after the incident, the Holy Spirit led me to take an in-depth study of David's path to become king of Israel.

The Holy Spirit wanted me to understand that doing a great job, working hard, and making personal sacrifices did not mean that I was ready for promotion. No one teaches us better about this life principle than David himself.

David's triumph over Goliath did not promote him to king immediately. Killing Goliath was David's introduction that would lead to the kingship, but not his crowning moment.

In First Samuel, Chapter 17, Israel and the Philistines had put the battle in array, army against army. For forty days the two armies lay encamped facing one another, each advantageously posted, but neither made a decision to begin fighting.

During this stand-off, David went to Israel's camp to deliver food to his brothers. Soon after he arrived, a Philistine champion, named Goliath, appeared. At his appearance, the men of Israel fled and were greatly afraid.

After Goliath left, the men began to talk amongst themselves of the king's reward for anyone who could kill him. The men spoke of how wonderful it would be to receive such a generous rewards package that consisted of great riches, the king's daughter in marriage, and their family made free in Israel.

David overheard the conversation and approached the men to confirm what should be done to the man who killed Goliath and take away the reproach from Israel. The men confirmed the rewards package.

As David reminisced how great it would be to win the mega million jackpot on Goliath's head and get rid of Israel's enemy, his brother Eliab approached.

Eliab told David, "I heard your conversation with the men. Why did you come here today and who is keeping your sheep? I know your pride and the naughtiness (wickedness) of your heart."

David responded, "What have I now done? Is there not a cause?" He turned from his brother and affirmed with the men again the reward for killing Goliath. With this second confirmation, he advised the king's inner circle that he wanted to fight Goliath, and they sent word to the king.

When Saul met David he saw a young, inexperienced boy who could not possibly take on a man of war like Goliath. Saul's dissatisfaction with his appearance did not deter David. He immediately ran through his resume. He highlighted his experience in killing a lion and a bear and with certainty pronounced that Goliath would be as one of them.

Grab a lesson from David's playbook. A promotional opportunity may arise, and others may not view you as promotion material; however, don't be afraid to share your accomplishments and how you can be a good fit for the position.

With his weapons of choice, five smooth stones, David whirled one of the stones at the head of Goliath, and he fell dead.

Shortly after this victory, Saul became jealous of David. His jealousy turned into rage, and Israel's mighty man of valor soon became a wanted outlaw.

David did not draw up an army to rise up against Saul or surprise him by some stratagem to end his tyrant leadership. In its place, he trusted God.

Instead of kicking it back in the king's palace, David found himself hiding from a mad king. Slowly, the shouts faded of Israel's jubilation over Goliath's death, and the anointing by the Prophet Samuel seemed nothing more than a distant memory.

Rather than nestling between silk sheets in the palace, David was forced to sleep with one eye shut and one eye open in dens and caves in the wilderness.

Before promotion comes humility. David was anointed king, but he was not ready for the throne, even though he killed a giant.

When his brother Eliab called out his pride, he brushed it aside. He was unaware of the pride that was looming in his heart.

It is not difficult to see how someone could blame Saul for David's dilemma, but it was the Lord behind the scenes orchestrating and, at times, allowing the events in his life to unfold.

Saul's pursuit to kill David was part of the refining process before his promotion to king. During this refining process, God used Saul to crush "the Saul" that was growing in David's heart.

We can't hurry the process to greatness. Patience must have its perfect work so that we may be perfect and entire lacking nothing.

Don't let the ungodly seduce you into following their path of unscrupulous tactics to attain promotions nor become dismayed by evil doers who are successful in getting ahead in the workplace.

With our faith in God, we will make it to the top in due season if we do not faint in the refining process.

FIVE

Positioned for Purpose

The Lord blesses us to acquire positions of power and influence on the job to help others.

Some years ago, the church I attended had a shelter on site, and many of the men from the shelter attended church services. While attending a function after church in our Fellowship Hall, one of the young men from the shelter approached me with an outstretched hand and said, "I am looking for a job; may I give you a copy of my resume?"

Suffice to say, he got my attention. As I stood reviewing his resume, he stated that the shelter is his current residence, but he wanted to get back on his feet. He described his previous work experience and talked about his career goals. I told him that I would see what I could do and would be back in touch with him.

The following day, I approached one of the managers that had several open positions in his department. He was on his way to a meeting, so I asked if I could talk with him as he walked.

As we walked, I told him that I met a young man who is looking for a job but doesn't have any technical experience. Due to his lack of technical experience, perhaps one of your entry-level positions would be a good fit for this young man. Starting him in an entry-level role would allow him to connect with one of your top performers and learn the job.

The manager replied, "My entry level technicians must have the ability to analyze and interpret technical procedures and engineer drawings, write reports, manage business correspondence, effectively present information, and respond to questions from groups of managers, clients, and customers. Is he a friend of yours?"

I replied, "No, I met him for the first time yesterday." He stopped dead in his tracks and said, "What did you say?" Immediately, I shoved the resume in his hand and ran.

After his meeting, he came to my office and said, "He is not qualified." Like the widow in the Bible who was persistent with her plea before the unjust judge, I pleaded why this man deserved a chance at the position.

After hearing my arguments, he said, "Send him to our recruiting agency and let them interview him. If he gets a pass from the agency, I will interview him."

When the agency interviewed the applicant, they were very impressed and recommended him for an entry-level position. With this recommendation, the manager hired the applicant as a contractor on a trial basis.

About two weeks after the young man began his job, the manager that took the risk could not believe how exemplary he was performing the job. Soon, he was offered a full-time position with the company and ultimately promoted to a management level position.

We must have a passion to use our position of power to help others in need by influencing the opinion of others.

SIX

Walk It Out

Undeniably, when I was searching for a job, it was a challenge to look for a job consistently and keep myself motivated to stay in the hunt.

Job searching can be a demanding and frustrating process. It requires tedious and meticulous hours to complete job applications or search for the right position, in a great location, with a competitive salary and benefits. Furthermore, the number of individuals competing in the job market for each open position is inordinate.

On one occasion, I spent about six hours applying online for jobs and was confident that I would hear from at least one of the companies. Regrettably, I did not get any bites or nibbles from any of my hard work.

Surprisingly, even if I wasn't sure I wanted the job I applied for, it was difficult to hear that I was not accepted to interview for the position. Increasingly, I became aware that feelings of rejection had the potential to yield a crop of self-pity and bitterness if left unchecked. I found praise to be the antidote for rejection; it kept my faith energized.

If you are searching for a job, don't give up. Irrespective of unanswered applications, interviews that do not materialize into a job offer, or lack of experience or education to compete for certain jobs, do not allow these barriers to paralyze you from pursuing the job God has for you.

In the course of preparing a lesson for my Bible study group, during the time I was looking for a job, I landed on the miracle Jesus performed for a man that had an infirmity for 38 years. His determination and persistence for a miracle gave me the encouragement I needed at the time to keep moving forward with my job search. The miracle is found in St. John, Chapter 5.

Jesus Christ, the enabler, meets a man who had an infirmity for 38 years. He meets this man at Jerusalem by the sheep market pool, which is called Bethesda. The pool had five large, long porches, where the sick waited for the angel to come down and trouble the water. Whosoever stepped into the pool, immediately after the angel troubled the water, would be healed.

It was at this pool that Jesus encountered "Mr. 38." This is a befitting name for this man, since he had been sick for 38 years.

At the pool lay a great multitude of impotent folks, which included the blind (sightless), halt (lame), and withered (paralyzed), waiting for the moving of the water.

If we look closely at the word impotent, it means "powerless." Powerless means void of strength or resources, lacking the authority or capacity to act. (See Webster's Dictionary.)

At the pool, a great multitude with various diseases and sicknesses waited for the angel, but Jesus went to the porch of the temple where the impotent lay.

When He saw Mr. 38 and knew that he had been in his condition for a long time, He said unto him, "Do you want to be made well?"

Mr. 38 answered, "Sir, I have no man when the water is troubled, to put me into the pool; but while I am coming, others step down before me blocking me from entering."

The question only required a one-word answer, "yes" or "no," but Mr. 38 wanted Jesus to know that the odds of getting into the pool were slim.

The question to Mr. 38 was about what he wanted to happen that day. It had nothing to do with yesterday or yesteryears. Jesus simply asked, "Do you want to be made well?" Did Mr. 38 answer Jesus? Of course he did; he said, "Maybe."

Mr. 38 failed to realize the power of his faith. Faith pushed him to go to the pool for a miracle. He was a dreamer; he saw himself healed. He witnessed the miracles of others, which gave him hope that one day, it would be his turn.

If you sit around thinking about how terrible the job market is, you will remain paralyzed right where you are.

For a fact, Mr. 38 had tried on several occasions to get himself into the pool. Whether he tried to roll himself into the pool or hold on to someone or cried for help, he let Jesus know that he had not been lying idle; he had tried but, at each try, he had failed.

If you want things to change in your life, you must do something. Those who expect nothing are never disappointed.

When Jesus asked Mr. 38, "Do you want to be made well?" I was surprised that he didn't scream, "Yes, yes, thank you for coming to help me get into the pool!" Instead, he started complaining. Discouragement convinced him that this year would be no different than last year or the years before. Discouragement also pointed out to Mr. 38 that this was the largest crowd ever and suggested to him that the person who brought him to the pool carelessly dropped him off and left him to fend for himself.

In the midst of this man's despair, he met Jesus Christ. Sadly, he couldn't strategize with Jesus on the best route to the pool because discouragement had beaten him down.

Mr. 38's doom and gloom response did not prompt Jesus to seek someone else who needed a miracle. Out of the great multitude of sick people gathered at the pool, it was Mr. 38's day for a miracle.

Jesus never acknowledged the man's excuses. Instead, He told Mr. 38 to rise, take up his bed, and walk. Jesus didn't help the man stand up; he stood on his own. Jesus wants us to hear his word and act upon it for results.

Stumbling blocks are stepping stones to success. Keep the faith, pick up your bed of excuses, and continue your job search. He has a job that is tailor made just for you.

SEVEN

Dare to Imagine

In the tale of "The Wizard of Oz," Dorothy and her motley crew wanted to find the Wizard of Oz in Emerald City.

On their journey to Emerald city, they encountered opposition from the wicked witch and her evil cohorts. The wicked witch's strategy was to use their insecurities to prevent them from reaching Emerald City. Each time the Wicked Witch created an obstacle to deter their journey, they persevered.

As they traveled down the yellow brick road, they spoke about what they lacked, why they needed to find the wizard, and what they wanted from him. The Scarecrow wanted a brain, the Lion wanted courage, the Tin Man wanted a heart, and Dorothy wanted to get home to Kansas. They believed that the acquisition of these "things" were essential to their success.

To their surprise, when they found the wizard, they discovered that he was simply human and had no great power. Nonetheless, they insisted that the wizard give them what they desired. Therefore, the Scarecrow was given a diploma to demonstrate that he was smart. The Tin Man received a clock so that he could hear a ticking sound from his chest. The Lion received a badge that represented bravery.

Although the wizard gave each of them something they could see and feel, they possessed everything they were seeking from the wizard.

The Scarecrow thought he needed a brain, yet he devised a strategy to outwit the wicked witch. The Tin Man thought he needed a heart, yet when adversity struck, he cried so hard that he rusted. The Lion thought he needed courage but, under pressure, he displayed the valor he believed he lacked. Dorothy wanted to go home to Kansas, but she was already in Kansas.

The wicked witch (satan) levees obstacles in our career path in an effort to discourage us from seeking promotions, a better job opportunity, or completing educational goals. If we manage our careers by seeking a path motivated by Godly goals, we can create the success we dare to imagine in our career.

Unlike Dorothy and her motley crew, we do not have to seek the advice from the wizard of this world. We are created in His image and in His likeness. You have everything that you could ever search for; Christ in you, the hope of glory.

PART TWO

KEEP IT REAL

EIGHT

The Dump

When I grew up in rural Virginia, we didn't have curbside garbage pickup. In its place, we had a community dump where you could discard trash and any other items that you did not want.

One man's trash became another man's treasure every time we went to the dump. We always found many treasures while rumbling throughout the dumpsite. Often we returned home with more items from the dump than we took to discard.

At the dump, there were times when I stumbled across something of great value and wondered why it was tossed away. Did they not know its value? Why didn't they give the item to someone rather than choosing to throw it in the dump?

In the workplace, there are gifted and talented individuals who are rejected by their managers, resulting in their dismissal from the company. These individuals are educated, brilliant, great problem solvers, have engaging personalities, know their field of expertise, and yet they are "thrown away."

Perhaps the manager did not take the time to properly train the employee in his or her role; therefore, the employee shipwrecked. Maybe the employee's performance shined too brightly, and the manager couldn't deal with the competition. Perchance the employee did not appear competent, and the manager believed the employee no longer added value. Perhaps the manager's vision changed, and the employee did not fit into the new vision.

Perhaps the manager and the employee consistently clashed, and the manager found it an unworkable situation.

Whatever the reason, managers have discarded many talented individuals in the "dump."

NINE

Did You See That?

Everyone has a built-in "inner language" that tells how to interpret what he or she sees and hears. Therefore, it is difficult to change perceptions.

Growing up with six siblings, I enjoyed the game called "Pass It On." The game required one person to whisper a sentence, phrase, or quote to a team member who then passed the whisper down the line. If the last person on the team could accurately repeat the information, the team received points. Most of the time, the sentence, phrase, or quote repeated by the person at the end of the line was greatly distorted.

What happened to the message? In most instances, the person repeated what they believed they heard, or they added their own spin on what they heard, and passed it along.

In the workplace, perceptions can lead to disagreements and unreceptive working relationships between individuals.

It is disappointing to hear a perception that someone has formulated about you that is incorrect, and you are helpless in trying to convince the person that he or she has the wrong perception. For some, what they believe they see or observe is their reality.

In the Old Testament, it was the perception of some, based on their "inner language," that caused them to believe that Saul, David's arch enemy, was a prophet because he was witnessed prophesying among the prophets.

After Saul whirled a javelin at David to kill him, David fled from Saul. Having escaped in the night, David did not go to Bethlehem to his kindred—or to any of the cities of Israel—but to Samuel, the prophet, and told him all that Saul had done to him. David sought Samuel for direction and instruction from God.

After learning that David fled with the aid of his wife, Michal, Saul sent messengers to Ramah to capture David. The prophets in Ramah, along with Samuel, were meeting at a location where they were praising and glorifying God.

When Saul's messengers came within their company, the Spirit of God came upon them, and they prophesied.

When Saul's messengers did not return after he had sent three companies of messengers, Saul went to Ramah to find David.

When Saul arrived in the company of Samuel and the prophets, the Spirit of God came upon him, and he began to prophesy. He spent the day and night in the presence of God with the prophets.

Onlookers knew that Saul was not a prophet but when they heard him prophesying, their *perception* was stronger than their reality. They asked among themselves, "Is Saul also among the prophets?"

Saul spoke God's Word when he prophesied, but his heart was far from thinking God's thoughts.

Saul went to Ramah to kill David. Saul's plan was interrupted when the Spirit of God immobilized him. God placed his spirit upon Saul to join in with the prophets so that David could have ample time to escape.

We cannot change anyone's perception, but we can change what others see by making a conscious effort to reflect His character in our interactions with others.

TEN

The Eyes Have It

Have you ever presented an exciting new idea only to receive a lukewarm or critical response?

While some may possess an inherent bias for structure and certainty, we should not be afraid to depart from the status quo.

There came a time when the children of Israel needed to move forward and possess the Promised Land, but they were afraid based on the evil report by ten of the twelve men Moses sent to spy the land of Canaan.

Ten spies advised Moses to scratch the idea of invading Canaan. Two spies (Joshua and Caleb) were adamant that Israel was more than able to possess the land and the time to do it was now.

Why did the ten spies want to avoid Canaan? The answer is found in Numbers 13:33, *"And there we saw the giants, the sons of Anak, which come of the giants: and we were in our own sight as grasshoppers, and so we were in their sight."*

The ten spies rejected Joshua and Caleb's plea to fight for the Promised Land; they were fearful Israel would be defeated.

Fear and unbelief prevented the ten men who spied the Promised Land from seeing God's plan and kept Israel from walking into their blessing.

It is significant to highlight that for forty days, the twelve spies Moses sent to spy Canaan roamed freely in enemy territory undetected and observed the same things in the land.

They went south to spy on the Amalekites and to the mountains and spied on the Hittites, Jebusites, and the Amorites. They spied on the Canaanites that dwelt by the sea and by the coast of Jordan. Not only did they roam freely from city to city, they had the audacity to steal fruit.

When the spies returned, they gathered Moses and the people to present their report. The ten fearful spies started the meeting on a positive note. Perhaps they had taken a course in Behavioral Management 101. They knew that it is better to start a meeting on a positive note when there is something unpopular to disclose.

The ten spies acknowledged that Canaan was a land that flowed with milk and honey, and they produced a cluster of grapes that were brought on a pole on the shoulders of two men.

Before the ten spies could speak against the land, they had to admit the truth. God did not lie about the land that flowed with milk and honey. The cluster of grapes was an ocular demonstration of its richness.

After the presentation by the ten spies, they urged Moses and the people not to go up against the inhabitants, because the people were strong, the cities were walled, and they saw giants in the land.

Upon seeing the people being persuaded by the evil report, Joshua and Caleb, two of the twelve spies, refuted the report, urging that they go up at once and possess the land.

Clearly, the children of Israel were homeless, and the ten fearful spies believed that it was better to stay out in the wilderness than to enter Canaan.

Canaan was a prime piece of real estate. There were vineyards, wells, streams, and rivers that flowed throughout the land. The pastures were filled with flocks and herds grazing. There were trees for shade and trees filled with fruit. There were houses built and fully furnished.

As the chaos grew out of control, Caleb took a bold move to still the people. Unwavering in faith, he admonished the children of Israel to go up at once and possess Canaan.

Indubitably, Caleb didn't want to go by himself; he was trying to get the people to see God as he saw Him. Regrettably, the children of Israel did not enter Canaan until 40 years later.

On the job, it can be a daunting task to influence others to appreciate an idea or viewpoint different than their own. When you receive a lukewarm or critical response to an idea or suggestion, don't discard it. Perchance it was not the right time or the right audience to act on it.

ELEVEN

Where Is the Love?

While working in a marketing department, two employees resigned at the same time due to the enormous workload, long hours, and what they believed to be a lack of appreciation for their hard work.

After their departure, I spent a lot of time thinking about leaving but never acted upon it. My excuses for not looking for another job were, "I didn't have time to look; the job is not that bad; the office is close to home; it's a good paying job." The excuses were endless.

Both positions were posted, but I never saw any movement or urgency by the department manager to fill the positions. About one month after the resignations, it was announced that the two vacant positions would not be back-filled and a decision would be made soon on how the workload would be reassigned within the department.

The day approached when the department manager released a plan of action for the vacant positions. To my surprise, I was tapped to assume both roles of the vacant positions. Upon hearing the decision, I started laughing. Yes, I laughed. To me, laughter was the appropriate response when you are told that you will be expected to perform three jobs with no pay increase and no help.

Companies are fighting for survival, and the reward you may find for doing a good job is more work. Was it a fair decision? "They" believed it was fair.

With my added duties, I devised a plan to take my three-tiered role and map it into one process in an effort to carve out a sense of sanity to the chaos.

My revised job responsibilities had many challenges, but I asked the Holy Spirit to show me how to manage my new workload. A few months later, with the help of the Holy Spirit, I had more free time than when I had one role.

Decisions made by management may not appear fair. You may feel that you got dumped on.

Whether it is an unpleasant business decision or a purposeful decision to push you out of the company, whatever He allows to happen, you can handle it.

TWELVE

The Devil Thought
He Had Me

Setup for failure is a strategy used in the workplace to make someone appear incompetent. Even if you know the person or persons that are manipulating events to set you up for failure, these attacks stem from the enemy. It is a spiritual battle.

Those who engage in setup for failure tactics are vicious and influential; therefore, you cannot combat the attacks with the arm of the flesh.

Permit me to remind you that fasting and prayer still work. More plainly, some calculated assaults will not dissipate without prayer and fasting.

Strategies used to make someone appear incompetent may include an assignment on a complex project, with ambiguity about the project goal and delivery, or tasked to create a presentation for a crucial meeting, or increased job responsibilities to a current strenuous workload. Often the employee is given little or no detail, vague instructions, and no assistance, all in an attempt to highlight one's ineptitude.

Similarly, a setup strategy may be to put you on the "hot seat" in a meeting by throwing you under the bus or picking apart your presentation in front of others. These schemes are designed to put you on the defense.

Don't be bewitched or bamboozled at the lengths to which the enemy uses individuals to play dirty. When the enemy attempts to use our haters to make our life a living hell, He will cause us to triumph. If God be for us; who can stand against us?

Some setup tactics are hard to recognize; therefore, we must be sober and vigilant, observing those subtle maneuvers. Walking in the Spirit allows us to see the enemy's plans, making us a victor and not a victim in his plot.

The enemy has no intentions of fleeing from us just because we are at work. As a matter of fact, the workplace gives him another avenue to wreak havoc.

Recently, a school teacher told me that she walked into her classroom and noticed dirty footprints tracked from the door across the classroom. However, when she looked more carefully, she observed that there were no footprints indicating that the person exited the classroom. Immediately, the Holy Spirit revealed to her that she needed to pray that demon out of her classroom. If this school teacher was not walking in the Spirit, she could have simply found a mop, cleaned up the mess, and given it no thought.

It's time to send the devil packing from your job. Daily attacks can drain us emotionally, mentally, physically, and spiritually. If you are dreading going to work or spending your day in a nervous state of frenzy, waiting for the next shoe to drop or losing sleep at night, this is torment!

Today, declare that you will not allow the devil to torment you any longer.

I have overcome many setup attempts and can boldly confess that God will have your back and gave you victories over your enemies.

When David saw Goliath tormenting the children of Israel, he cried, "Who *is* this uncircumcised Philistine, that he should defy the armies of the living God?" When David went to fight Goliath, he had no fear. Immediately, he declared, "Game over!"

David placed one smooth stone in a slingshot and aimed it at Goliath's head. The stone alone did not contain the power to kill Goliath. The presence of the Lord of hosts, the God of the armies of Israel in the force of the stone, killed Goliath.

When the enemy comes in like a flood, the Lord of hosts will thwart every setup strategy aimed at you. We are His children and He will give His angels charge over us to keep us in every test and trial we face.

We are more than conquerors. The devil was defeated at Calvary by the One who bore the three nails on a tree.

THIRTEEN

God Did It

Unavoidable, there will be spiritual battles and scrimmages in the workplace. When the Lord fights our battles, we must elude the pitfall of accepting the credit for the victory. A prideful heart can lead to a beat down at the next battle if we place our confidence in our abilities.

At each battle, we must consult the Lord for a winning strategy. We cannot assume that the same strategy should be used for every battle, even if it was successful the last time we used it. Joshua, Moses' successor, reinforces this life lesson.

Joshua and the children of Israel were riding an emotional high after their monumental victory in Jericho.

After winning the battle at Jericho, Joshua sent men to spy out the city of Ai, their next conquest.

When the men returned from spying Ai, the men told Joshua, "This is an easy battle; we've got this one." They advised Joshua to send only two or three thousand men to take the city and let the rest of the soldiers sit this one out.

Joshua adhered to the advice of the spies and sent 3000 men to fight Ai. At the battle, Ai chased Israel fiercely, and they fled for safety.

When the men returned to camp running from their enemy, the hearts of the people melted. Joshua tore his clothes and fell to the ground on his face before the ark of the Lord, and the elders of Israel mourned with him.

The children of Israel were stunned. They had a phenomenal victory at Jericho and could not fathom why they suffered such a devastating defeat at Ai.

One might conclude that Ai was able to defeat Israel because it's not always the size of the dog in a fight but the size of the fight in the dog. However, there is a substantive explanation why Israel suffered a defeat; it had nothing to do with Ai's military might.

What was the difference between the battle at Jericho and the battle at Ai? First of all, when Joshua sent the spies into Jericho, they reported, "Truly the Lord has delivered into our hands all the land: for even all the inhabitants of the country do faint because of us."

When the spies returned from Ai, they reported, "Let not all the people go up. Only let about two or three thousand men smite Ai, because it's only a few of them."

There is a glaring difference in the attitude of the men who spied Jericho and the men who spied Ai. The spies who returned from Jericho reported that the Lord had delivered the land into their hands. The spies who returned from Ai reported, "We can take care of them."

How many times has the devil tempted us to make decisions based on what we can see? The spies looked at their enemy and came to the conclusion that they could beat them. They were so confident in their own fighting abilities that they excluded God.

Israel's defeat at Ai knocked the wind out of their sails; they had no strength to speak.

Adversity has a way of delivering blows that deplete our strength. Isaiah 40:29 reminds us that *the Lord gives power to the faint and to them that have no might, He increases strength.*

You may have started a new job or a new role in which you were certain God directed you into acquiring; however, trouble has reared its ugly head, and you are questioning if you made the right decision. Relax, take a deep breath, and ask the Lord to give you direction. Trouble is not always a sign that something is wrong; trouble is also a sign that something is right.

Joshua pointed the finger at God for the defeat. He wanted to know how Israel could be successful again in the face of their enemies and what will other nations do when they hear that Israel's God allowed one of their enemies to defeat them?

Joshua was devastated that Israel got whipped. He questioned why the Lord blessed them at Jericho and then disgraced them at Ai. He told the Lord, "Our enemies will hear of this, surround us, and then what will you do unto your great name?" The battle at Ai was only a defeat in Joshua's eyes, not God's.

God revealed to Joshua the reason for the defeat at Ai. After Joshua removed the evil from the camp, the Lord instructed him to go up to battle against Ai. God provided Joshua with a new strategy, not the same one implemented at Jericho. The strategy led to Israel's successful defeat of Ai.

When God gives you a victory, don't leave him on the sidelines at your next battle. Moreover, don't take any credit for the win—God did it.

PART THREE

REBOOT

FOURTEEN

The Power of One Talent

"For the kingdom of heaven is as a man traveling into a far country, which called his own servants, and delivered unto them his goods. And unto one he gave five talents, to another two, and to another one; to every man according to his several ability; and straightway took his journey.

Then he that had received the five talents went and traded with the same, and made them other five talents. And likewise he that had received two, he also gained other two. But he that had received one went and digged in the earth, and hid his lord's money.

After a long time the lord of those servants cometh, and reckoneth with them. And so he that had received five talents came and brought other five talents, saying, Lord, thou deliveredst unto me five talents: behold, I have gained beside them five talents more. His lord said unto him, well done, thou good and faithful servant: thou hast been faithful over a few things, I will make thee ruler over many things: enter thou into the joy of thy lord.

He also that had received two talents came and said, Lord, thou deliveredst unto me two talents: behold, I have gained two other talents beside them. His lord said unto him, well done, good and faithful servant; thou hast been faithful over a few things, I will make thee ruler over many things: enter thou into the joy of thy lord.

Then he which had received the one talent came and said, Lord, I knew thee that thou art a hard man, reaping where thou hast not sown, and gathering where thou hast not strawed: And I was afraid, and went and hid thy talent in the earth: lo, there thou hast that is thine.

His lord answered and said unto him, Thou wicked and slothful servant, thou knewest that I reap where I sowed not, and gather where I have not strawed: Thou oughtest therefore to have put my money to the exchangers, and then at my coming I should have received mine own with usury.

Take therefore the talent from him, and give it unto him which hath ten talents. For unto every one that hath shall be *given, and he shall have abundance: but from him that hath not shall be taken away even that which he hath." Matthew 25:14-29*

When God looks at us, He sees things that others may ignore. He looked at David and saw a king inside a shepherd boy.

When God did not move the prophet Samuel to anoint any of Jesse's sons that paraded before him, he asked Jesse, "Do you have any more children?"

We are God's offspring. There are many "selves" within us that live dormant, untapped, and unused. God sees potential that may not be yet visible to us. There is more inside of you than that which is evident on the outside.

What we want to accomplish and who we want to be have unlimited possibilities. What will you do with the talents God has invested in you?

In the parable of the talents, the master gave one servant five talents, another servant two, and another servant one talent. He distributed the number of talents according to what he felt each servant could handle.

The servant that was given one talent took it and hid it in the ground. He could not comprehend the power of the seed in the one talent.

The master never expected the servant with one talent to produce five. When we do not capitalize our potential, we hide our talent because it is the safe thing to do rather than moving beyond our comfort zone.

God has made each of us unique and different than any other person on the face of the earth. In spite of our uniqueness, we can be drawn into the trap of wanting to be like someone else. Few people like themselves as they are; they like seeing themselves in someone else.

There is extraordinary talent in the workplace, and amongst such talent, insecurities can loom large. Being "you" is more potent than conforming to what you think others may want you to be.

We will never discover whom we were meant to be if we allow others to define us. Likewise, we cannot determine what we can do by using what someone else has done to measure our capability.

While the master distributed talents according to the abilities of his servants, God views success as making the most of our abilities.

The servant with the one talent could not move beyond the limitations of his self-perception. He wanted to play it safe and refused to take a risk. He was convinced he would fail; he didn't try. Never underestimate the power of one—you!

FIFTEEN

No Right Way
to
Do the Wrong Thing

Have you ever made a questionable decision to advance your career because you got tired of waiting on God to bless you? Have you taken matters into your own hands and, in the process, cut some moral corners?

Taking matters into our hands can delay blessings and cause us to reap the consequences of our choices; just ask David.

"And David said in his heart, I shall now perish one day by the hand of Saul: there is nothing better for me than that I should speedily escape into the land of the Philistines; and Saul shall despair of me, to seek me any more in any coast of Israel: so shall I escape out of his hand.

And David arose, and he passed over with the six hundred men that were with him unto Achish, the son of Maoch, king of Gath.

And David dwelt with Achish at Gath, he and his men, every man with his household, even David with his two wives, Ahinoam the Jezreelitess, and Abigail the Carmelitess, Nabal's wife.

And it was told Saul that David was fled to Gath: and he sought no more again for him.

And David said unto Achish, if I have now found grace in thine eyes, let them give me a place in some town in the country that I may dwell there: for why should thy servant dwell in the royal city with thee?

Then Achish gave him Ziklag that day: wherefore Ziklag pertaineth unto the kings of Judah unto this day.

And the time that David dwelt in the country of the Philistines was a full year and four months." 1 Samuel 27:1-7

There came a time when David became fed up with Saul's relentless pursuit of his life. It appeared that God was not coming to rescue him, so David decided to take matters into his own hands.

Fear can lead to bad decisions based on a one day thought process. What is your one day fear?

David's heart convinced him that one day Saul was going to kill him. Fear at that moment in his life was his reality. In essence, his fear was stronger than his faith.

David was an outlaw running for his life with 600 gang bangers and their families. He was tired of ducking and hiding and wanted a normal life. With no end in sight to Saul's madness, he focused on his present, not his future. He could not fathom life getting any better.

One day while in a state of despair, his heart convinced him that he needed to make a drastic move. Not only did he want to get away, he needed a long term solution that would cause Saul to stop pursuing him.

Finally, a brilliant plan came to mind: if he relocates to Gath and lives with Israel's enemy, the Philistines, this would solve all of his problems.

Who could blame David for seeking a way out of his dilemma? When the king of a nation wanted him dead, how could David escape? Think about it, a king had alerted an entire nation to be on the lookout for David. He couldn't show his face downtown or uptown.

David was particularly proud of himself for thinking of such a unique hiding place for he and his entourage. As it went, once Saul was told that David fled to Gath, he never sought to hunt him again. On the surface, it appeared that David had outsmarted his enemy.

God was moving too slow for David, so he made a life-altering decision for himself and those who accompanied him, based upon his feelings.

It can be tempting to take matters into our own hands if we perceive that God is not taking any action.

After being anointed by the prophet, Samuel, David was enrolled in a rigorous training curriculum, "The Making of a King." Before honor is humility; Samuel left that part out of David's anointing ceremony.

The flesh does not like it when God starts doing stuff without its input or permission. Although we want to grow and mature in Christ, we would like to be kept abreast of everything; just in case we don't like a certain test or trial, then we can opt out.

Achish, the king of Gath, was pleased to have David in his country. After all, Israel's most valiant warrior was not too shabby of a neighbor. The king offered David a place in the city to live; however, he asked the king to be granted a parcel of land away from the city so that he would be removed from the king's watchful eye. The king gave David land in Ziklag.

David arrived in Gath with a deceptive plan to execute. After settling in Ziklag, he needed to provide food and necessities for the people. To accomplish this, he and his men invaded the Geshurites, Gezrites, and the Amalekites. He robbed and killed the inhabitants for food and supplies. During each raid, he killed everyone to make certain no one could report that he was the assailant.

To make sure he convinced King Achish that he had turned his back on Israel; he gave some of the spoil from the raids to the king.

Upon seeing the loot, King Achish asked David, "Whom did you raid today?" He replied, "Against the south of Judah."

The king replied, "You have caused Israel to utterly abhor you, and therefore you shall be my servant forever."

David's reaction to King Achish's remark, that he would be his servant forever, did not trouble his spirit. How could David serve an ungodly master? Do you see the subtle spiritual deterioration taking root?

David's deception became his reality. He rationalized his behavior because the Geshurites, Gezrites, and Amalekites were Israel's old enemies; they were getting what they deserved. David did not realize that there was no right way to do the wrong thing.

David flew under the radar until, one day, the Philistines gathered to make war with Israel. When David heard that the Philistines were going to make war with Israel, he wanted to fight with the Philistines.

As the Philistines reviewed the final strategy plans as they approached Israel, the lords of the Philistines discovered that David and his men were bringing up the rear. The Philistines were appalled that David and his men would have the audacity to be marching with them to fight against their own nation and their own people. They refused to believe that David had deserted Israel.

The lords of the Philistines immediately confronted King Achish and asked, "Is not this David, of whom they sang one to another in dances saying, Saul slew his thousands and David his ten thousands? Make this fellow go home. We don't want to be in the heat of the battle against Israel and he decides to reconcile with his master. We don't want David to turn on us and kill us."

King Achish stood alone in defending his decision to include David but to no avail. The lords of the Philistines were adamant that he make David and his men leave. Consequently, Achish told David that he must turn back and could not go with them to fight against Israel.

At that announcement, David should have started shouting and praising God that he did not have to fight Israel, but, instead, he challenged the decision. David was angry that he had been told to stand down. He asked Achish, "What have I done?"

Achish did not back down when David challenged his decision. In a forceful tone, he told him, "You are not going."

The king urged David and his men to get up early in the morning, as soon as they saw light, and depart. David was very displeased that he could not fight with the Philistines.

Could David mess up God's plan for him to rule over Israel? No—he could not. As a matter of fact, Saul couldn't kill David, but at this particular time, he believed that Saul could kill him; that's why he fled to Gath.

It was God's job to ensure that David did not derail His plan. It was never David's responsibility to make sure he was crowned king.

Although David was "saved by the bell," his bad decisions soon caught up with him, and he had to own the consequences.

When David and his men returned to Ziklag, they found their town burned to the ground and not a trace of their wives and children, nor their flocks and herds. It was an unmitigated disaster.

David's first response was grief. He didn't just grieve, he led the grieving. *"Then David and the people that were with him lifted up their voices and wept, until they had no more strength to weep." (1 Samuel 30: 4)*

David moved to Gath to get rid of Saul, but he did not comprehend that his trials by the hand of Saul were preparing his heart to rule over Israel.

God allowed David to make the choice to leave Israel, but that was not His choice.

Every trial on the job is not from the devil; it could be God orchestrating events. We must trust God to work out His plan; we can't rush or rewrite the plan. He knows what He is doing, even when others on the job appear to be excelling and you appear to be stuck.

We cannot make bad decisions and expect God to follow us. There is no right way to do the wrong thing.

SIXTEEN

A Do Over

Over the years, I have made a host of mistakes and blunders in the workplace. Without a doubt, you can choose to change your behavior and regain the trust of others regardless of the mistakes you have made.

In the book of First Samuel, Chapter 30, David suffered the consequences of his choice to move to Gath, but he was redeemed by the hand of a merciful God.

David's resolution to get back the trust of others came when he and his men returned to Ziklag and found the city burned with fire; and their wives, sons, and daughters were taken captive. He was greatly distressed, for the people spoke of stoning him because the souls of the people were grieved.

For the first time in over a year, David realized that his actions in Gath contributed to the dilemma he faced upon returning home to Ziklag. He messed up, but he also realized that God could help him pursue and recover all that had been taken from him and his men.

There was no time to contemplate what he wished he woulda, coulda, or shoulda done differently. How much precious time we waste frustrated by what has already happened that we cannot possibly change.

David's men wanted to kill him. At this threat, he could have chosen to fight the men, beat himself up for the damage that he had caused, or run away from the problem. None of these choices could rebuild the city or bring back the women and children who were taken captive.

Instead, David went to the person who had delivered him from a lion, a bear, a giant, and a mad king. David inquired of God as to whether he should pursue the Amalekites. God told David to pursue, and that he shall without fail recover all.

If you want God's help in your situation, you must ask. God is not keeping a scorecard of your mistakes. When you ask God for forgiveness, He will forgive you and remember your sin no more. The only people who can fish for your past mistakes are you and the people who refuse to let you forget.

When God told David he would recover all, two hundred of David's men were so faint that they could not follow David. The remaining four hundred that went with him didn't go because they trusted him; they went because they did not want their families killed or made slaves.

David and his men pursued the Amalekites to recover their families. In the course of their pursuit, they encountered an Egyptian slave who led them to the Amalekites' camp, where their wives and children were being held captive. When your back is against the wall, God will provide a "ram in the bush."

When David and his men reached the camp of the Amalekites, they were dancing, eating, and drinking because of the great spoil they had taken.

There may be people who believe your mistakes have immobilized or destroyed you, but don't underestimate the power of a mighty God.

Let your enemies rejoice at what appears to be your demise. What they don't know is that Jesus is the resurrection and the life. When you trust God, He can and will resurrect you in the presence of your enemies.

The Amalekites were great in number. The Bible describes them as "spread abroad upon all the earth," but David and his men went into the enemy camp and recovered all.

It makes no difference if others cause us pain, or we make decisions causing self-inflicted heartache or pain. Regardless of whether the adversity comes from without or within, God is a present help in the time of trouble.

SEVENTEEN

Benchwarmers

There have been times in my career in which I was part of a team but was not invited to play in the game. If you are forced to watch your team perform from the sideline, do not allow their actions to impede your growth.

When the quarterback is sacked during a game, he doesn't walk off the field. He picks himself up and runs another play. This is the level of perseverance God wants us to display at work.

When your team or department makes a conscious decision to keep you sitting on the sideline and refuses to let you in the game, take the opportunity to recalibrate and reinvent yourself.

When I was benched, no one payed me attention or cared about what I was doing, because they believed they had taken me out of the game. In place of murmuring and complaining, I formed new alliances in other departments within the organization.

Moreover, I took the initiative to learn how each department was aligned within the organization and became involved in new supportive roles.

Quickly, my interest in other roles outside of my department increased my understanding of business processes. As a result, I gained valuable knowledge and insight in how each department added value in accomplishing the company's goals.

If you find yourself benched from the game, continue your high level of performance by showing up to work on time and working diligently on any tasks assigned to you. This is not the time to despise this season in your career. Your attitude will determine your comeback.

Since the devil will be coming at you from all angles to shatter your self-worth while you are benched, it is vital that you quench every negative thought with the Sword of the Spirit.

In my benched season, I redefined myself and my job. This move led me to lead a project in which, years later, my colleagues continue to talk about its success.

God has blessed us with extraordinary gifts and talents and, in due time, He will allow those gifts and talents to be made known to others. Your gifts will make room for you and bring you before great men!

EIGHTEEN

Some Eggs Just Can't Be Cracked

After slaying Goliath, David became captain of King Saul's army; he got a promotion.

In First Samuel, Chapter 18, David found himself caught up in a contentious work environment created by a group of women who recorded a song that was more favorable to David, and sang it before King Saul. Saul was offended by the song and believed the people were "falling hard" after David.

As captain over Israel's army, the position gave David insight on how to command Israel's vast army, of which he would be commander in chief later.

David was enjoying his new job until the women came out of the cities of Israel, singing and dancing, to meet King Saul and his army, who were returning from a victory over the Philistines.

The women sang that Saul had slain his thousands, and David his ten thousands. From that incident, Saul looked on David with suspicion.

A contentious working relationship can begin with a simple, no harm intended remark or action that can cause one to be the receiver of unkind treatment. One song turned Saul into a mad king.

Although David was unsuccessful in convincing Saul that he was not his enemy, David continued to behave wisely.

When the opportunity presented itself for David to slay Saul, he chose not to touch the Lord's anointed.

When Saul learned that David could have slain him but spared his life, this act of kindness did not deter Saul from seeking to kill him.

The solution to working harmoniously in a contentious work environment is to behave oneself wisely. Sometimes no matter how much you conduct yourself in a positive manner, those who formulate a negative opinion of you will not change their minds.

Individuals who choose to hold onto resentment and nurse their wounds are eggs who just can't be cracked.

PART FOUR

ENDING WISDOM

NINETEEN

Unscripted Praise

The power of praise caused the children of Israel to conquer Jericho. In the book of Joshua, Chapter 6, we encounter the siege of Jericho by the children of Israel, led by Joshua, Moses' successor.

When the children of Israel approached Jericho, they found it tightly locked down; none went out, and none came in.

The city of Jericho had fortified walls up to 25 feet high and 20 feet thick. Soldiers who stood guard on top of the walls could see for miles. Jericho was a symbol of military power and strength; the Canaanites considered it invincible.

The Canaanites believed their enemies could not prevail against a walled city. They did not view the children of Israel as a threat. After all, they were not trained warriors but freed slaves from Egypt.

To conquer Jericho, military preparations were not necessary. Instead, the ark of God was carried by the priests around the city once a day for six days, attended by the men of war. This did not intimidate the Canaanites; in any case, no one has ever captured or defeated a city by walking around it.

God needed the children of Israel to know that it would be by faith, not force, which would cause them to capture Jericho. On the seventh day, the children of Israel walked around Jericho seven times. When the people shouted, as the priests blew the trumpets, the walls of Jericho fell flat.

Praise allowed the children of Israel to enter the promised land. Likewise, praise undergirds our faith and sets the stage for God to move on our behalf.

Apostle Paul declared in Acts 20:24, *"None of these things move me, neither count I my life dear unto myself, so that I might finish my course with joy, and the ministry, which I have received of the Lord Jesus, to testify the gospel of the grace of God."* None of these things (whatever is thrown at us in the workplace) have the power to move us into a state of panic or distress.

As we learned from Joshua and the children of Israel at Jericho, praise is the antidote to immobilize individuals and situations which appear invincible.

A praise break before an important presentation or crucial meeting refreshes our focus and thoughts and primes our spirit to hear the counsel of the Holy Spirit.

When Clark Kent needed to become Superman to defend humanity against threats, he used a phone booth to make a quick change into his Superman suit.

When I need quick wisdom and guidance, or want to bind demonic activity, I seek Superman (the Holy Spirit). If a private, secluded area is unavailable, I get "my praise on" in a restroom stall. Without making an audible sound, I speak in my heavenly language, as I pray and praise. When I finish praising, I wipe the tears, flush the toilet, wash my hands, and return to work.

We have the authority to pull down strongholds on the job and everything that exalts itself against the knowledge of God.

Taking the time to put on the garment of praise will cause walls of opposition to crumble.

The Lord does not want us stressed at work. When you need a quick pick-me-up, find a restroom stall and offer up some unscripted praise.

TWENTY

Zip It Up

"At that time Berodach-baladan, the son of Baladan, king of Babylon, sent letters and a present unto Hezekiah: for he had heard that Hezekiah had been sick.

And Hezekiah hearkened unto them, and showed them all the house of his precious things, the silver, and the gold, and the spices, and the precious ointment, and all the house of his armour, and all that was found in his treasures: there was nothing in his house, nor in all his dominion, that Hezekiah showed them not.

Then came Isaiah the prophet unto king Hezekiah, and said unto him, What said these men? and from whence came they unto thee? And Hezekiah said, They are come from a far country, even from Babylon.

And he said, What have they seen in thine house? And Hezekiah answered, All the things that are in mine house have they seen: there is nothing among my treasures that I have not showed them.

And Isaiah said unto Hezekiah, Hear the word of the Lord. Behold, the days come, that all that is in thine house, and that which thy fathers have laid up in store unto this day, shall be carried into Babylon: nothing shall be left, saith the Lord.

And of thy sons that shall issue from thee, which thou shalt beget, shall they take away; and they shall be eunuchs in the palace of the king of Babylon." 2 Kings 20:12-18

Hezekiah's desire to impress a heathen prince caused him to be more transparent than he should have been with his personal business.

He gave the messengers sent by the King of Babylon a tour of his palace and treasures so that they would make a favorable report to their master—that he was a great king.

The Lord was displeased with Hezekiah's actions and sent the prophet Isaiah to let him know that everything he bragged about in his kingdom would be carried into Babylon; nothing would be left.

Some individuals love to make themselves the center of attention at work. Their personal life is an open book to all who do and do not want to read it. The danger in sharing all of you—or being loosey-goosey—is that it can make you an easy target for your haters to use what they know about you to sabotage your career.

James 3:5-6: "The tongue is a little member; how great a matter a little fire kindleth. The tongue among our members can defile the whole body."

Before you blab all of your business, ask yourself, *will my life at work change for the better or worse or will it remain the same if I tell my business?* Your answer to this question should assist you in assessing what is safe to disclose.

There will be occasions in which an illness, or some other significant circumstance, will make it impossible to keep some personal problems private, particularly if it has the potential to impact your attendance or job performance.

Sometimes you may face issues in which you are seeking advice or just need to vent. If this is the case, create a small circle of friends with which you can share personal issues to gain advice or a listening ear.

Rule of thumb: what happens away from work should stay away from work.

Nasty Grams

Some employees are more comfortable saying what they really want a person to know through an email rather than mustering up the courage to speak face-to-face with the person.

I label emails that are sent for the sole purpose of getting someone told off, or setting the record straight, as nasty grams. Nasty grams are always a "no-no" in the workplace.

If you perceive that an email contains incorrect information, or the content of the email places you in an unfavorable light, do not respond in a defensive manner or attempt to set the record straight. A face to face conversation is more appropriate. This will also eliminate engaging in a war of words through email.

A nasty gram provides your company with documentation of inappropriate behavior that could come back to bite you in the butt.

Similarly, whenever you are tempted to counter a zinger (jab) in an email by returning a zinger, don't do it. You can't throw stink bombs and expect the scent not to get on you.

If you have any reservation about the information that you have placed in an email, don't send it. Instead, pause, take a deep breath, and save the email to send later.

Most often, once you've had time to walk away, regroup your thoughts, and calm down, you will most likely decide to discard it or rewrite it in a more appropriate tone.

TWENTY-TWO

We Hang Our Own

One of the most painful revelations in the workplace is to encounter betrayal at the hand of church folk.

If the church is the light that the world should see, a city that is set on a hill that cannot be hid, our actions should match the profession of our faith.

Putting on a Sunday face with tears streaming down one's cheeks, hands lifted toward heaven worshipping the Father, and the persona of an angel do not impress God if our hearts are black.

Moreover, any spiritual gains made on Sunday can be erased by Monday if we do not allow the Word of God to change our worldly ways (profanity, lewd behavior, lying, manipulation, deception).

The workplace is a mission field, and how we conduct ourselves may be the only sermon that some will hear.

Respond to your responsibility as an ambassador for Christ. The harvest is plenteous, but the laborers are few.

TWENTY-THREE

Home Alone

Ephesians 4:14—"That we henceforth be no more children, tossed to and fro, and carried about with every wind of doctrine, by the sleight of men, and cunning craftiness, whereby they lie in wait to deceive."

God does not need to give us visions, signs, and wonders every day to let us know that He is with us. He would be a lousy Father to forget one of His children. Relax, God will not pull a home alone on you.

There will be times when your career goals appear to be out of reach, or perhaps you are overlooked, again, for a position or promotion. Don't get distracted by how things appear. God knows everything that concerns you.

When things appear delayed or you feel stuck, don't become frustrated in the process. Resist the temptation to hurry things along.

The process may appear slow, but allow God to prepare, teach, and humble you at every stage of refinement. This preparation period is crucial for the challenges you will face up the road.

TWENTY-FOUR

See You at the Top

It is not a sin to desire success. It becomes sin when the methods and motives to acquire success are not aligned with God's Word.

With success comes responsibility and visibility. Those who climb to the top by divisive means may find that they must continue using the same strategy in order to stay at the top.

At the top, failure to perform usually leads to two options: demotion or termination. For most, it is the latter.

God does not prepare us at the top. He prepared David to be a warrior while in his role as a shepherd. He used the bear and the lion to teach him how to fight a giant.

When David brought food and supplies to his brothers on the battlefield, he had no idea that he was going to fight a giant that day. Victory is inescapable when preparation collides with opportunity.

When we get to the top, we are charged with implementing the things we learned on our climb to the top. Often, the Lord does not promote us into positions of power until we have been tested and tried in the fire. David didn't get to the throne until several years after he was anointed by Samuel.

Out of our experiences, He transforms us into candidates for promotion.

The hell on your job just might be the fiery furnace by which God prepares you for greatness. During your fiery trials, your behavior and choices may not mimic what you know about God, or you may not consistently display Christ like character in your actions or attitude. Don't beat yourself up; it's part of the process of dying to self.

Along with the fiery trials, you may experience long periods in which you feel alone, but don't forget that He will never leave or forsake you.

Saul's pursuit to kill David birthed some of the most incredible writings by David in the book of Psalms.

If Saul had not pursued David, he would not have written in Psalm 27: *"The Lord is my light and my salvation; whom shall I fear? the Lord is the strength of my life; of whom shall I be afraid? When the wicked, even mine enemies and my foes, came upon me to eat up my flesh, they stumbled and fell.*

Though a host should encamp against me, my heart shall not fear: though war should rise against me, in this will I be confident. One thing have I desired of the Lord, that will I seek after; that I may dwell in the house of the Lord all the days of my life, to behold the beauty of the Lord, and to enquire in his temple.

For in the time of trouble he shall hide me in his pavilion: in the secret of his tabernacle shall he hide me; he shall set me up upon a rock. And now shall mine head be lifted up above mine enemies round about me: therefore will I offer in his tabernacle sacrifices of joy; I will sing, yea, I will sing praises unto the Lord."

If Saul had not pursued David, he would not have written in Psalm 31: *"In thee, O Lord, do I put my trust; let me never be ashamed: deliver me in thy righteousness. Bow down thine ear to me; deliver me speedily: be thou my strong rock, for a house of defence to save me.*

For thou art my rock and my fortress; therefore for thy name's sake lead me, and guide me. Pull me out of the net that they have laid privily for me: for thou art my strength. Into thine hand I commit my spirit: thou hast redeemed me, O Lord God of truth."

If Saul had not pursued David, he would not have written in Psalm 34: *"I will bless the Lord at all times: his praise shall continually be in my mouth. My soul shall make her boast in the Lord: the humble shall hear thereof, and be glad.*

O magnify the Lord with me, and let us exalt his name together. I sought the Lord, and he heard me, and delivered me from all my fears. They looked unto him, and were lightened: and their faces were not ashamed.

This poor man cried, and the Lord heard him, and saved him out of all his troubles. The angel of the Lord encampeth round about them that fear him, and delivereth them. O taste and see that the Lord is good: blessed is the man that trusteth in him."

At the present time, tests and trials seem painful rather than pleasant, but later it yields the peaceful fruit of righteousness to those who have been trained by it.

End of the Rainbow

In Christ, it doesn't matter if your job is mopping floors or the President of the company, He will use situations and circumstances at work to sharpen your spiritual weapons. Throughout the years, I frequently revisited the fine points of the vision mentioned in my Introduction. At the beginning of my journey, the vision was the rope of hope I held as I navigated through challenges in the workplace.

I know first-hand what it feels like to be in an unending cycle of storms. I have also witnessed the mighty hand of God during the storms. It can't rain all the time; the sun will shine again.

One of the most beautiful sights to see after a storm is a rainbow. Who can resist standing in awe of a beautiful, multicolored arch that is breathtaking to behold. Its bright colors demand our attention, because it illuminates the sky in such a magnificent display.

After your storm, there will be a rainbow. He will reward those who diligently seek Him. He has a pressed down, shaken together, and running over blessing just for you.

God will always cause you to navigate through any storm on the job when you put your trust in Him. He secured this victory for you over two thousand years ago with three nails and a tree.